Tips for Blogging: Google AdSense Approval of an Article

Asif Mehmood

Copyright © 2024 Asif Mehmood

All rights reserved

The characters and events portrayed in this book are fictitious. Any similarity to real persons, living or dead, is coincidental and not intended by the author.

No part of this book may be reproduced, or stored in a retrieval system, or transmitted in any form or by any means, electronic, mechanical, photocopying, recording, or otherwise, without express written permission of the publisher.

ISBN-13: 9798329154399
ISBN-10: 1477123456

Cover design by: Art Painter
Library of Congress Control Number: 2018675309
Printed in the United States of America

Contents

Title Page	
Copyright	
Tips for Blogging: Google AdSense Approval of an Article	1
Understanding Google AdSense Requirements	2
Creating High-Quality Content	3
Originality and Uniqueness	4
Informative and Valuable	5
Well-Structured and Readable	6
Visual Content	7
Optimizing Blog Design and Navigation	8
Responsive Design	9
Clear Navigation	10
Fast Loading Speed	11
Implementing Essential Pages	12
About Page	13
Privacy Policy Page	14
Contact Page	15
Ensuring Compliance with AdSense Policies	16
Prohibited Content	17
Ad Placement	18

Building Organic Traffic	19
Keyword Research	20
Quality Backlinks	21
Social Media Promotion	22
Regularly Updating Content	23
Monitoring and Analyzing Performance	24
Conclusion	25

Tips for Blogging: Google AdSense Approval of an Article

In the evolving landscape of digital marketing, getting your blog approved for Google AdSense is a crucial step towards monetizing your content. AdSense approval can significantly increase your blog's revenue, but the process requires attention to detail and adherence to Google's guidelines. This comprehensive guide provides actionable tips to help you secure AdSense approval for your articles, ensuring your blog stands out and meets all necessary requirements.

Understanding Google AdSense Requirements

Before diving into specific tips, it is essential to understand the basic requirements set by Google AdSense. These requirements are designed to ensure that the ads placed on your site provide value to both advertisers and users. The primary criteria include:

Creating High-Quality Content

Quality content is the cornerstone of any successful blog. To increase your chances of AdSense approval, focus on the following aspects of content creation:

Originality and Uniqueness

Ensure all your articles are original and free from plagiarism. Use plagiarism checkers to verify the uniqueness of your content. Original content not only attracts more readers but also aligns with Google's quality standards.

Informative and Valuable

Your content should provide value to readers. Address common questions, offer solutions to problems, and provide in-depth analysis on topics relevant to your niche. The more value you provide, the more likely readers are to engage with your blog.

Well-Structured and Readable

Organize your content with headings, subheadings, and bullet points to enhance readability. Use short paragraphs and simple language to make your articles accessible to a wider audience. A well-structured article is easier to read and keeps readers engaged longer.

Visual Content

Incorporate images, videos, and infographics to complement your text. Visual content not only makes your articles more appealing but also helps illustrate key points, making your content more engaging and informative.

Optimizing Blog Design and Navigation

A well-designed blog with intuitive navigation enhances user experience and is crucial for AdSense approval. Pay attention to the following elements:

Responsive Design

Ensure your blog has a responsive design that works seamlessly on both desktop and mobile devices. A mobile-friendly blog improves user experience and is favored by Google's algorithms.

Clear Navigation

Create a clear and intuitive navigation structure. Use menus, categories, and tags to organize your content logically. A well-organized blog helps users find information quickly and keeps them engaged.

Fast Loading Speed

Optimize your blog for fast loading speeds. Compress images, use caching plugins, and choose a reliable hosting provider to ensure your site loads quickly. Fast-loading sites offer a better user experience and are more likely to rank higher in search results.

Implementing Essential Pages

Certain pages are essential for AdSense approval as they demonstrate the legitimacy and transparency of your blog. Ensure your blog includes the following pages:

About Page

An About Page provides information about the blog and its authors. It helps build credibility and trust with your audience. Include details about your mission, vision, and the purpose of your blog.

Privacy Policy Page

A Privacy Policy Page is a must-have for AdSense approval. It informs users about data collection practices and how their information is used. Use online privacy policy generators or consult legal advice to create a comprehensive policy.

Contact Page

A Contact Page makes it easy for readers and potential advertisers to reach you. Include a contact form, email address, and social media links to ensure accessibility.

Ensuring Compliance with AdSense Policies

To avoid rejection, ensure your blog complies with all AdSense policies. Regularly review the AdSense program policies and make necessary adjustments to your blog. Key areas to focus on include:

Prohibited Content

Avoid publishing content related to violence, adult material, copyrighted material, and other prohibited categories. AdSense has strict guidelines on acceptable content, and violating these can lead to rejection or account suspension.

Ad Placement

Follow the guidelines for ad placement to avoid excessive or intrusive ads. Ensure ads are placed in a way that does not disrupt the user experience. Google recommends a balance between content and ads to maintain a user-friendly site.

Building Organic Traffic

A blog with high organic traffic is more likely to get AdSense approval. Implement effective SEO strategies to improve your search engine rankings and attract more visitors.

Keyword Research

Conduct thorough keyword research to identify terms and phrases relevant to your niche. Use tools like Google Keyword Planner, Ahrefs, and SEMrush to find keywords with high search volume and low competition. Integrate these keywords naturally into your content to improve visibility.

Quality Backlinks

Acquire quality backlinks from reputable sites in your niche. Guest posting, collaborations, and content syndication are effective ways to build backlinks. High-quality backlinks signal to Google that your site is trustworthy and authoritative.

Social Media Promotion

Promote your content on social media platforms to increase visibility and drive traffic. Engage with your audience on Facebook, Twitter, Instagram, and LinkedIn to build a loyal readership and encourage shares and interactions.

Regularly Updating Content

Regularly update your blog with fresh content to keep your audience engaged and improve your search engine rankings. Google favors sites that are consistently updated with new, relevant content. Set a content calendar and stick to a regular posting schedule.

Monitoring and Analyzing Performance

Use tools like Google Analytics and Google Search Console to monitor your blog's performance. Analyze metrics such as page views, bounce rate, and average session duration to understand how users interact with your site. Use these insights to make data-driven decisions and continuously improve your blog.

Conclusion

Securing Google AdSense approval requires a combination of high-quality content, a well-designed blog, compliance with policies, and effective SEO strategies. By following the tips outlined in this guide, you can enhance your blog's appeal to both users and Google, increasing your chances of AdSense approval and ultimately, your blog's profitability.

www.ingramcontent.com/pod-product-compliance
Lightning Source LLC
Chambersburg PA
CBHW072057230526
45479CB00010B/1125